Tucson Teddy
Takes a Trip

Catalina Island

By Dennis & Phyllis Seawright

Graphic Design by Kellie Shelton Sherrill

One day Tucson Teddy said,

"It's time for another trip."

Catalina Island seemed like fun...

...and he could sail there

on a ship.

Tucson Teddy loves to travel

and to see the sights,

so in the town of Avalon

he'll be exploring days and nights.

So first he got a shovel, then a yellow bucket too. Now he was ready to play on the beach, like he always wanted to do. He'd dig a few holes, make a sand castle or two, then off he'd go, he had so much more to do.

Teddy wished to see some bison
but they were far away.
So he would have to play instead
with a toy one made of clay.

High up on his list to see

the beautiful Casino,

standing by the sea.

The top floor is for dancing

and downstairs is a show.

If it played "Kung Fu Panda,"

he'd be sure to go.

Out at Descanso Beach there were kayaks for him to use. But if he had stayed on shore there are other things to choose.

Teddy found a wall of rock that was there for him to climb. He scrambled up so very fast, he reached the top in record time.

Now he decided it was time for a thrill,

so he rode a special bus to the top of the hill.

He got buckled up and when he was ready,

down the zip line flew Tucson Teddy!

When lunch time finally
rolled around,
his tummy made a hungry sound.
He thought of Eric's hot dogs,
which were so very near...

...but he ended up with

Fish & Chips,

that was also on the pier.

After lunch he took a ride

that really was a hoot.

The boat pulled him high into the sky

in a beautiful parachute.

And then he took a ride

upon another boat.

It can go under water

when it doesn't want to float.

He rode beneath the water clear,

and when it was just right...

...Teddy was with the fish below,

and giggled with delight.

Now he thought he'd play some golf

but since he was so small,

he'd try his luck at miniature golf

and surely have a ball.

He hoped he'd hit a hole-in-one

for that would be a treat,

but he hit the ball so very hard

it landed in the street.

To see more of the Island,

he'd need to climb hills

oh so steep.

So instead he hopped into

a shiny new tour jeep.

The tour made a stop at the Airport-in-the-Sky, and there he saw a funny plane that he would love to fly.

Up at the Nature Center
with an eagle by the door,
Teddy learned of plants and birds
and the people who lived there
long before.

There was a special garden
that was also on his list,
but once inside he saw a plant
that showed him what he missed.

The cactus was before him

and reminded him of home.

It was time for Teddy to go there,

no more time for him to roam.

Even though Tucson Teddy

was going to sail away,

he knew he'd return to Catalina

on another day.

The  End

To our grandchildren Mike, Jenny, Katie,
Lauren, Emily and our great-grandson Cole.

Phyllis and Dennis Seawright were born and raised in
Southern California where they met in high school,
married and raised three children.
They now reside in Avalon on Catalina Island.

Made in the USA
Charleston, SC
16 January 2017